My First Acrostic

Birmingham
& The West Midlands

Edited by Donna Samworth

First published in Great Britain in 2011 by:

 Young**Writers**

Remus House
Coltsfoot Drive
Peterborough
PE2 9BF
Telephone: 01733 890066
Website: www.youngwriters.co.uk

Foreword

The 'My First Acrostic' collection was developed by Young Writers specifically for Key Stage 1 children. The poetic form is simple, fun and gives the young poet a guideline to shape their ideas, yet at the same time leaves room for their imagination and creativity to begin to blossom.

Due to the young age of the entrants we have enjoyed rewarding their effort by including as many of the poems as possible. Our hope is that seeing their work in print will encourage the children to continue writing as they grow and develop their skills into our poets of tomorrow.

Young Writers was established in 1990 to nurture creativity in our children and young adults, to give them an interest in poetry and an outlet to express themselves. This latest collection will act as a milestone for the young poets and one that will be enjoyable to revisit again and again.

Contents

Worthen CE Primary School, Worthen

The Poems

Danyaal

D utiful

A mazing

N ice

Y outhful

A dorable

A rtistic

L ovely.

Danyaal Ahmed (5)
Anderton Park School, Sparkhill

Laiba

L iveliness

A dventure

I nvestigation

B alloon

A crostic.

Laiba Farooq (3)
Anderton Park School, Sparkhill

1

Moosa

 anner

 bedient

 bservation

 ensible

 ctive.

Moosa Khan (3)
Anderton Park School, Sparkhill

The Wonderful Child

 arvellous

 dorable

 ively

 rtistic

 ntelligent

 ind

 dventurous.

Malaika Ali (4)
Anderton Park School, Sparkhill

Abid

A bid is going to school

B all

I n the garden playing

D og.

Abid Ali (4)
Anderton Park School, Sparkhill

All About Me!

E xcellent in making my brothers do things for me

I am a good girl

M y parents love me so much

A nd all my friends love me so much

A nd all my teachers love me

N o sorry, I don't have time for any questions.

Shaila Nitasha Eimaan (3)
Anderton Park School, Sparkhill

3

Eleanor

E I like *eggs*

L I like *l*ollies

E I like elephants

A I like apples

N I love *N*anny

O I like oranges

R I like *r*abbits.

Eleanor Matthews (5)
Broadheath CE Primary School, Lower Broadheath

Yasmin

Y I like *y*oghurt

A I like *a*pples

S I like *s*wimming

M I love my *m*ummy

I I like *i*ce cream

N I love my *n*anny.

Yasmin Martin (5)
Broadheath CE Primary School, Lower Broadheath

Elliot

E I like elephants

L I like lions

L I like lizards

I like ice cream

O I like oranges

T I like tigers.

Elliot Whittaker (5)
Broadheath CE Primary School, Lower Broadheath

Cat In The Hat

C at in the hat sat on a marvellous mat

A nd then rat came to the mat, together they went

T o the hut.

Diana Amirkhanyan (6)
Chad Vale Primary School, Edgbaston

Weather

Wind and sun, snow and rain,

Every day is not the same.

All of us like sunshine

Temperature's high, those are fine.

Heat makes my roses grow and

Every day we hope for better

Rather than it getting wetter!

Abigail Dawn Parker (6)
Chad Vale Primary School, Edgbaston

Birthdays

Birthdays happen every year

It is my favourite time of year

Running and jumping in the garden

This is the best party

Happy time for everyone

Don't want this day to end

All this cake for me

Yeah, presents!

Say thank you for coming to everyone.

Jai Johal (6)
Chad Vale Primary School, Edgbaston

Songs/Dancing

S unny days make me happy

O nce upon a time

N ight-time is it?

G rass is green

S kateboards are cool.

D ancing is fun

A ustralia is sunny

N ana is magic

C hristmas Santa is nice

I n a rock concert

N o water

G ardens are fun because you can play in them.

Joseph Ryan Argus (6)
Chad Vale Primary School, Edgbaston

Spring

S unshine

P laying in the park

R unning rabbits

I ce cream and treats

N ests and Easter eggs

G rowing apple blossom.

Grace Cawsey (5)
Chad Vale Primary School, Edgbaston

Princess

P recious

R eally pretty

I n a castle

N ice and little

C inderella in a castle

E xcellent dress

S inging

S weet songs.

Maheen Malik (4)
Chad Vale Primary School, Edgbaston

Myself

N ever eats chocolate

A lways behaves well

T ired every day

A lways goes to bed late

S its on the comfy chair

H elpful every day

A lways eats melon.

Natasha Golding (5)
Chad Vale Primary School, Edgbaston

Myself

A ctive

M agic

A mazing

A rtistic

Y oung

A wesome.

Amaaya Mirza (6)
Chad Vale Primary School, Edgbaston

Myself

R eally likes ice cream

I am very rich

S ometimes I go to bed late

H elpful to my parents

I make good choices.

Rishi Ramchandani (6)
Chad Vale Primary School, Edgbaston

Myself

E very day I ride my bike to school

V ery helpful every day

E very day I help my dad.

Eve Yarker (5)
Chad Vale Primary School, Edgbaston

Myself

A lways active

R unning every day

Y ou're very helpful

A lways doing the right thing

N ever goes to bed early.

Aryan Gohil (6)
Chad Vale Primary School, Edgbaston

Myself

E very day I come to school on time

S ome days I play football

A ll day I do my homework.

Esa Alam (6)
Chad Vale Primary School, Edgbaston

Myself

L eon loves chips

E very Monday I eat all my breakfast

O n Friday I go to Asda

N o chocolate.

Leon De Medeiros (5)
Chad Vale Primary School, Edgbaston

Myself

K ind and helpful

A mazing and fabulous

R un really fast

T idy and fast

H elpful to my friends

I ntelligent in the morning

K nowledgeable to my mum.

Karthik Ganesan (6)
Chad Vale Primary School, Edgbaston

Myself

J umping

E xcellent

S mart

S ensible

E xciting.

Jesse Muogbo (5)
Chad Vale Primary School, Edgbaston

Myself

H elps people with their bags

A lways does different things

R eally helpful to my teachers

S ometimes I like to play with my friends

I am kind to everybody

M akes different things

R eally good at wordsearches

A ctive and fun

N ever calls out.

Harsimran Kang (5)
Chad Vale Primary School, Edgbaston

Myself

R ich

O verjoyed

H andsome

A mazing

N ice.

Rohan Sangha (5)
Chad Vale Primary School, Edgbaston

13

Myself

 ctive

N ice

V ocal

I mportant

R eliable.

Anvir Buray (5)
Chad Vale Primary School, Edgbaston

Myself

R eliable

O utstanding

M agic

A mazing

N ice.

Roman Shokar (5)
Chad Vale Primary School, Edgbaston

Myself

S mart

A mazing

C aring

H appy

V ocal

I nteresting

R ich.

Sachvir Cooner (5)
Chad Vale Primary School, Edgbaston

Myself

N ice

A mazing

M agical

I nteresting

R eliable

A ctive

H elpful.

Namirah Khan (5)
Chad Vale Primary School, Edgbaston

Myself

O utstanding

S mart

C aring

A mazing

R ich.

Oscar Piotrowski (6)
Chad Vale Primary School, Edgbaston

Myself

M agical

I nteresting

C heerful

H elpful

E nergetic

L ovely

L ively

E xciting.

Michelle Wen (5)
Chad Vale Primary School, Edgbaston

Myself

M akes wonderful cakes

A lways is amazing

R eally rich

T ries my best

H elpful always

A mazing and fabulous.

Martha Wright (5)
Chad Vale Primary School, Edgbaston

Football

F ootball is good

O ctopuses play football very well

O ld people can still play football

T eddies can still play football

B abies like to dribble

A nybody likes to watch football

L ollipops like to watch football too

L ions love to play football.

Ned Harvey (6)
Crowle CE First School, Worcester

Sticky Toffee

S mell that fantastic smell

T aste the stickiness

I 'm in heaven

C areful, you need to suck it

K eep chewing

Y ummy, that tastes good

T ry the terrific toffee

O pen up the wrapper

F ind your favourite flavour

F inish it fast

E njoy it all while it's there

E very bit has gone!

Stella Taylor (7)
Crowle CE First School, Worcester

Tilly

T oday I went swimming with my daddy

I am always good in school

L ovely handwriting in her stories

L ovely behaviour every day

Y es she is always delightful.

Tilly Turnbull (7)
Dixie Grammar Junior School, Wellsborough

Triceratops

T ries to stay away from meat eaters

R uns away from predators

I t only eats plants

C ould put horns in a T-rex's tummy

E xceptionally heavy

R oughly fights with other dinosaurs

A lways shy

T o meet friends he roars

O f course children are afraid of it

P uts his big feet in mud.

S uper sharp horns.

Thomas W Cross (7)
Dixie Grammar Junior School, Wellsborough

Danika

D oes her best

A nd every day she smiles

N ever cruel to children

I s smart in school

K ind and caring in maths

A very special helper for teachers.

Danika Nuttall (7)
Dixie Grammar Junior School, Wellsborough

Lewis

L ikes to eat food

E ats a lot of fish flakes

W ants me to feed him

I s always swimming around

S ees my face a lot in the glass bowl.

Owen Marlow (7)
Dixie Grammar Junior School, Wellsborough

Mark

M agnificent dad

A very special helper

R uns as fast as a cheetah

K icks the ball hard.

Alfie Madden (7)
Dixie Grammar Junior School, Wellsborough

William

Will always do my best

I am a good boy

Likes fish and chips

Loves birthday treats

Is helpful at home

Always kind to others

Makes lots of LEGO.

William Clarke (7)
Dixie Grammar Junior School, Wellsborough

Robyn

Runs until she's out of breath

Often naughty but always good

Beautiful girl

Yes I am great at maths

Now I am learning at school.

Robyn Walker (7)
Dixie Grammar Junior School, Wellsborough

21

Buddy

B rown spaniel puppy

U seful at running

D efinitely my best pet

D oes sleep on my bed

Y es, always comes when I call him.

Isabel Koster (7)
Dixie Grammar Junior School, Wellsborough

Matthew

M y party was yesterday

A t bedtime I read for fourteen minutes

T oday is good and I like maths

T oday I will go to Beavers

H appy, helpful and healthy

E xcellent at maths and loves dinosaurs

W ill have fun at school today.

Matthew Coutts (7)
Dixie Grammar Junior School, Wellsborough

Emily

E nergetic in PE

M oves fast at running

I mportant little girl

L oves writing and swimming

Y es, she is always delightful.

Emily Clement (7)
Dixie Grammar Junior School, Wellsborough

Lexie

L exie loves lollipops

E xcellent at maths

eX tremely good at maths

I s a good girl

E xcellent at comprehension.

Lexie Deer (6)
Dixie Grammar Junior School, Wellsborough

Oscar

O h what a kind boy

S uper maths king

C oncentrates well

A ccurate maths

R uns quickly.

Oscar Bunting (6)
Dixie Grammar Junior School, Wellsborough

Edan

E xcellent at comprehension

D oesn't like rainy days

A lways fun

N ever naughty.

Edan Hale (6)
Dixie Grammar Junior School, Wellsborough

24

Jenny

J olly good in science

E xtra good at maths

N ow I like tennis

N ever naughty in PE

Y es she is getting better at comprehension.

Jennifer Smart (6)
Dixie Grammar Junior School, Wellsborough

Toby

T ries his best

O ften I am good, sometimes I am naughty

B eautiful boy

Y es he is always a delightful boy.

Tobylee Salisbury (6)
Dixie Grammar Junior School, Wellsborough

Animals

A pe
N ight monkey
I nsects
M onkey
A nt
L ion
S pider.

Frederick Powner (4)
Dixie Grammar Junior School, Wellsborough

Animals

A lligator
N ight monkey
I insects
M onkey
A nts
L ion
S wan.

Archie Davenport (4)
Dixie Grammar Junior School, Wellsborough

Animals

A lligator
N ight monkey
I nsects
M eerkat
A nt
L adybird
S wan.

Ava Whetstone-Magee (4)
Dixie Grammar Junior School, Wellsborough

Animals

A nt
N octurnal
I nsects
M oth
A lligator
L ion
S pider.

Peter Morton (4)
Dixie Grammar Junior School, Wellsborough

Animals

A ntelope

N ewt

I nsects

M oth

A pe

L ion

S wan.

Freddie Clarke (4)
Dixie Grammar Junior School, Wellsborough

Animals

A nt

N ight monkey

I guana

M oth

A pe

L ion

S wan.

Nigel Underwood (5)
Dixie Grammar Junior School, Wellsborough

Animals

A nt

N ight monkey

I guana

M ouse

A lligator

L ion

S eal.

Jacob Trollope (5)
Dixie Grammar Junior School, Wellsborough

Animals

A nt

N ewt

I guana

M eerkat

A pe

L ion

S pider.

Alyssa Richichi (5)
Dixie Grammar Junior School, Wellsborough

Animals

A nt
N ewt
I guana
M oth
A pe
L ion
S wan.

Holly Davies (5)
Dixie Grammar Junior School, Wellsborough

Animals

A nt
N ight monkey
I guana
M eerkat
A pe
L ion
S wan.

Megan Franklin (5)
Dixie Grammar Junior School, Wellsborough

Animals

A nteater
N ewt
I nsects
M ouse
A nt
L ion
S wan.

William Pearce (5)
Dixie Grammar Junior School, Wellsborough

Animals

A nt
N ewt
I nsects
M ouse
A pe
L ion
S eal.

Jovan Dosanjh (4)
Dixie Grammar Junior School, Wellsborough

Animals

A nt
N ewt
I guana
M ouse
A pe
L ion
S wan.

Imogen Dracup (5)
Dixie Grammar Junior School, Wellsborough

Winter

W e are throwing snowballs
I magine I was skiing
N ext to the high hills
T he children are snowboarding
E very morning I wake up and there is snow
R udolph has a shiny nose.

Ted Davies (6)
Dixie Grammar Junior School, Wellsborough

Winter

When it is cold I snuggle up to my blanket

Icicles are pointy

Now we can sledge

The snow is white and soft

Everyone is happy

Rudolph has a shiny nose.

Alayna Friston (6)
Dixie Grammar Junior School, Wellsborough

Winter

We are going sledging

Ice is freezing

New snow is fluffy

Try to make a snowman

Everyone is celebrating Christmas

Robins in a tree.

Eleanor Bee (6)
Dixie Grammar Junior School, Wellsborough

Winter

W e see snowflakes

I ce is cold

N ow the snow falls on the ground

T he snow is white

E ach child has a toy at Christmas

R ush downstairs to open them.

Emily Jackson (5)
Dixie Grammar Junior School, Wellsborough

Winter

W e make a snowman

I cicles are freezing

N ice, cold winter

T hen we go inside

E veryone is happy tonight because Santa is coming

R ush outside to play.

Daisy Wilebore (6)
Dixie Grammar Junior School, Wellsborough

Winter

W e are playing in the snow

I magine there is an igloo in the North Pole

N ext I am drinking hot chocolate

T he people are ice skating

E veryone is waiting for Christmas

R obins tweet at the window.

Emily Cutler (6)
Dixie Grammar Junior School, Wellsborough

Winter

W hen I go out we make a snowman

I like singing in the snow

N ext I throw snowballs at Daddy

T his ice is freezing and cold

E very time I go outside I see icicles

R obins are singing in the tree.

Francesca Bowman (5)
Dixie Grammar Junior School, Wellsborough

Winter

W e are cold

I go indoors

N orth wind is freezing

T he ice is slippy

E verything is snowy

R obins eat seeds.

Annabel Koster (6)
Dixie Grammar Junior School, Wellsborough

Winter

W e make a snowman

I like playing in the snow

N ext I put the snowman's scarf on him

T he snow is white

E verything is frosty

R ush inside to get warm.

Guy Kibble (6)
Dixie Grammar Junior School, Wellsborough

Winter

We are ice skating

I like sledging in the snow

N ice Christmas dinner

T he snow is falling down

E veryone is making a snowman

R udolph is coming tonight.

Maddison Bolsover (5)
Dixie Grammar Junior School, Wellsborough

Winter

We are going to make a snowman

I cicles falling down onto the ground

N ow we are going to have a Christmas dinner

T hen we are going to have a Christmas pudding

E veryone is excited that Christmas is coming

R osy cheeks are red and hot.

Hannah Clarke (5)
Dixie Grammar Junior School, Wellsborough

Winter

We saw a robin

Imagine I saw Santa

Next I made a snowman

The snowman is big

Everyone likes the snowman

Reindeer fly across the sky.

Flora Easton (6)
Dixie Grammar Junior School, Wellsborough

Winter

We can see a robin

In the igloo is an eskimo

Next go inside to keep warm

The wind is cold

Everyone is throwing snowballs

Run away to keep safe.

Rio Naik (5)
Dixie Grammar Junior School, Wellsborough

Winter

W hite snow is falling

I made an igloo

N ext I have a snowball fight

T hen we are freezing

E verything is white

R eindeer come tonight.

Joseph Blunt (5)
Dixie Grammar Junior School, Wellsborough

Winter

W e make a snowman

I like to skate on ice

N ext I like to throw a snowball

T hen the snowball hits my daddy

E veryone is laughing

R osy cheeks.

Beth Morton (5)
Dixie Grammar Junior School, Wellsborough

Winter

W e like playing in the snow

I like making snowmen

N orth wind makes me cold

T he snowman is good

E veryone is ice skating

R obins come out in winter.

Samuel Ashley (5)
Dixie Grammar Junior School, Wellsborough

Emily

E xcited at home.

M oody when my brother says no.

I mpressed when I pass my spellings.

L ovely all the time.

Y ummy my tummy is angry when I don't get my yummy dinner.

Emily Harrison (6)
Guardian Angels Catholic Primary School, Shard End

Ava

A mazing always

V ery pretty girl

A wesome all the time.

Ava Casey (6)
Guardian Angels Catholic Primary School, Shard End

Niamh Fardy

N ice

I mpressive

A mazing

M ini

H elpful

F aithful

A fraid

R oyal

D elightful

Y ummy.

Niamh Fardy-Hall
Guardian Angels Catholic Primary School, Shard End

Cody

C ats are amazing

O ur house is nice

D addy is lovely

Y appy Cody is one.

Cody Green (5)
Highters Heath Community School, Kings Heath

Peter

P eter is friendly

E xciting

T errific

E xcellent

R unning.

Peter Hands
Highters Heath Community School, Kings Heath

Eman

E man is healthy

M agic

A mazing

N ice.

Eman Mohammed
Highters Heath Community School, Kings Heath

Jodie

J elly is yummy

O ranges are delicious

D inosaurs are funny

I love jelly

E lephants are very, very, very super.

Jodie Hollinshead
Highters Heath Community School, Kings Heath

Nadim

N umber clubs are weird

A weird boy is Nadim

D addy is the best

I am Nadim

M y name is Nadim.

Nadim Ahmed (6)
Highters Heath Community School, Kings Heath

Demi

D ogs are excellent

E ggs are my favourite

M y mum is fantastic

I am healthy.

Demi Green
Highters Heath Community School, Kings Heath

Charlie

C hocolate

H at

A mazing

R an

L oves

I ce cream

E nd of poem.

Charlie Swinbourne (5)
Highters Heath Community School, Kings Heath

Adam

A mazing

D inosaur

A ct

M ist.

Adam Pola
Highters Heath Community School, Kings Heath

Adam

 book

D oors

A badge

M e.

Adam Ali-Dad
Highters Heath Community School, Kings Heath

Lacie

L acie is brilliant

A bout

C hildren

I nsect

E veryone.

Lacie Hallard
Highters Heath Community School, Kings Heath

Ellady

E gg
L eg
L ovely
A mazing
D inosaur
Y ay!

Ellady Newsome (6)
Highters Heath Community School, Kings Heath

Tyler

T ray
Y ellow
L eg
E gg
R obot.

Tyler Jeffrey (5)
Highters Heath Community School, Kings Heath

47

Zara

Z oo
A cat
R at
A nt.

Zara Rani
Highters Heath Community School, Kings Heath

Gruffalo

G ruffalo is so big

R un if you see him

U gly, smelly Gruffalo

F luffy fur

F ast running

A lways nasty

L oves Mummy and Daddy

O range eyes.

Willow Hodgson (7)
Holmer Lake Primary School, Telford

Gruffalo

igantic jaws

uns away when he's scared

gly, slimy, green warts at the end of his nose

urry, fluffy body

rightening sharp teeth

mazing animal

oves to eat chocolate-covered mice

range lightning eyes.

Chloe Gibbons (6)
Holmer Lake Primary School, Telford

Gruffalo

igantic feet

oars lovely

gly wart

urry body

lappy ears

mazing purple prickles

oud stomps

range lava eyes.

Emily Elliott (6)
Holmer Lake Primary School, Telford

Gruffalo

G oggly eyeballs

R oars loudly

U tterly knobbly knees

F rightening creature

F iggy furry body

A rgues with himself

L ingering breath

O range eyes.

Callum Wiggin (6)
Holmer Lake Primary School, Telford

Gruffalo

G igantic teeth

R uns very fast like the wind

U gly big wart

F ur is soft

F ur all over his body

A mazing ears

L oves his food

O range lava eyes.

Ella Rowntree (6)
Holmer Lake Primary School, Telford

Gruffalo

G igantic ears

R oars super loud

U gly body

F rightful Gruffalo

F urry, fluffy body

A mazing teeth

L oves to eat toast

O range cut eyes.

Kaitlin Bailey (6)
Holmer Lake Primary School, Telford

Gruffalo

G reedy and lazy

R oars loudly

U gly, smelly, black tongue

F rightened of the mouse

F urry, fluffy body

A lways greedy

L oud roars

O range eyes.

Rhys Edwards-Barnes (7)
Holmer Lake Primary School, Telford

Gruffalo

G reedy, fat monster

R oars loudly

U pset tummy

F rightening

F at

A lways red bloodshot eyes

L ikes mouse on toast

O range eyes.

Joshua Lloyd (6)
Holmer Lake Primary School, Telford

Gruffalo

G igantic jaws

R oars loudly

U gly, smelly, black tongue

F rightened of the mouse

F ast it runs in the night to catch a mouse

A mazing purple prickles

L oves to eat mouse on toast

O range eyes.

Shannon Fradgley (6)
Holmer Lake Primary School, Telford

Environment

E co-friendly is

N ice and healthy

V ery good for the Earth

I t's very clever too

R ecycle all our waste

O rganising the rubbish

N ever forget

M ake sure

E verything is done to

N ot damage or hurt

T he environment.

Jacob Surgenor (7)
Holmer Lake Primary School, Telford

Gruffalo

G ruffalo is mean

R ound eyes like the moon

U gly wart

F urry tummy

F ur is prickly

A nice mouse

L oves his mum and dad

O pens doors.

Lillie Peachey (6)
Holmer Lake Primary School, Telford

Jungle

J umping jolly frogs jumping over the river

U p in the sky birds are tweeting

N ever go near the terrible lion, he will eat you for his tea

G orillas are punching their chests very hard

L ions are roaring for their tea

E lephants are stamping very loud.

Kyle Till (6)
Holmer Lake Primary School, Telford

Jungle

J umping jaguars

U p in the trees swinging monkeys

N asty snapping crocodiles

G reedy tiger

L ovely hummingbird

E vil lions laughing at their prey.

Chloe Bailey (6)
Holmer Lake Primary School, Telford

Jungle

J umping monkeys climbing about

U p above butterflies flying in the sky

N aughty crocodiles in the river

G rowling lions looking for their prey

L oud elephants stamping their feet

E xcited snails slithering about.

Lauren Taylor (6)
Holmer Lake Primary School, Telford

Jungle

J umping red frogs

U nder a log are ants eating

N aughty monkeys breaking branches

G iraffes eating leaves

L azy lions laughing

E normous elephants stomping.

Cameron Conner (6)
Holmer Lake Primary School, Telford

Monkeys In The Jungle

Moves fast

Opens his big eyes

Noisy monkey

King of the jungle

Eats bananas

Yummy, yummy.

Jessica Jackson (6)
Holmer Lake Primary School, Telford

Scary Tiger

Tries to hide in the grass

In and out of the grass

Growls at others

Eats meat

Roar, roar, roar.

Jasmine Hesbrook-Key (6)
Holmer Lake Primary School, Telford

Tiger

T iptoeing in the grass

I n and out it goes

G rowls and roars

E ats lots of animals

R uns very fast.

Harry Jones (5)
Holmer Lake Primary School, Telford

Enormous Bear

B ig growling bear

E ars always listening

A lways hungry

R un away fast.

Aysha Taylor (6)
Holmer Lake Primary School, Telford

Funny Monkey

M akes a funny noise

O range eyes

N oisy little monkey

K ing of the jungle

E ats bananas

Y ummy, yummy.

Molly Davies (6)
Holmer Lake Primary School, Telford

Jungle Animals

T earing at meat

I n the long grass

G rowling

E normous claws

R un fast.

Ernests Petrovskis (5)
Holmer Lake Primary School, Telford

Jungle Bear

B ig brown bear

E ats the berries

A lways asleep

R uns very fast.

Harry Bates (5)
Holmer Lake Primary School, Telford

Chloe

C ute

H appy heart

L ovely

O bserving

E veryone's friend.

Chloe Wilcox (4)
Lickhill Primary School, Stourport On Severn

Tyler

T rendy

Y ummy

L azy in the morning

E xcellent

R unning, racing Tyler.

Tyler Bray (5)
Lickhill Primary School, Stourport On Severn

Ruby

R uby runs

U p the castle

B ecause I like to run like

Y ou!

Ruby Dudley (4)
Lickhill Primary School, Stourport On Severn

Neve

N ice

E xcellent

V ery magic

E njoys drawing.

Neve Farebrother (4)
Lickhill Primary School, Stourport On Severn

Iqram

I ce cream

Q uick at . . .

R unning

A mazing

M agic.

Iqram Chowdhury (5)
Lickhill Primary School, Stourport On Severn

Lucy Gore

L ovely

U p the ladder

C up of tea

Y o-yo

G orgeous and fantastic

O n the top

R ub names off the board

E njoys the fun.

Lucy Gore (4)
Lickhill Primary School, Stourport On Severn

Leah

L ovely

E ats apple

A nd oranges

H elpful.

Leah Davies (5)
Lickhill Primary School, Stourport On Severn

Warren

W acky

A mazing

R udd

R unning

E xcellent

N ice.

Warren Rudd (4)
Lickhill Primary School, Stourport On Severn

Libby

L ovely

I like horses

B ouncy

B army

Y ummy.

Libby Minor (4)
Lickhill Primary School, Stourport On Severn

Eleanor Jones

E ats Quavers

L oves running

E xcellent

A lover of literacy

N othing's ever the matter with me

O ffer people to play my game

R elaxing girl.

J uice, orange juice is the best

O ctagon group is the best and I'm in it

N ever ever give up at work

E xpert in getting stars

S mart.

Eleanor Jones (7)
Lickhill Primary School, Stourport On Severn

Rebecca Stock

R eally tall

E xplains troubles

B irthday on the 24th January

E ats lollipops

C ool

C an jump onto my bed

A ctive

S uper

T aught how to write

O utside I play on my climbing frame

C ooks cakes

K ind.

Rebecca Stock (7)
Lickhill Primary School, Stourport On Severn

Neve Hackett

ice

E ver so helpful

V ery beautiful

E njoyable

H appy

A mazing

C lever

K ind

E xcellent

T errific

T hinker.

Neve Hackett (6)
Lickhill Primary School, Stourport On Severn

Lauren Kirk

L ovely

A fantastic girl

U seful

R eally great

E xciting

N ice

K now my ten times tables

I eat chips and fish

R eady for work

K eep turtles.

Lauren Kirk (7)
Lickhill Primary School, Stourport On Severn

Khyati

K ind

H appy

Y ellow when I am cold

A rtistic

T hinker

I ndian.

Khyati Bhardwaj (7)
Lickhill Primary School, Stourport On Severn

Tyler Spencer

T all

Y oung

L azy

E vil

R ule my family

S even

P lay up

E nergetic

N ice

C ool

E verton

R ule!

Tyler Spencer (7)
Lickhill Primary School, Stourport On Severn

Milan Krivosic

M arvellous

I tchy

L azy

A mazing

N ice

K icking

R ich

I rresistable

V ictorious

O utrageous

S ensational

I nteresting

C hampion.

Milan Krivosic (6)
Lickhill Primary School, Stourport On Severn

Millie

M ad

I nteresting

L ovely

L oud

I ncredible

E xcellent.

Millie Mezzone (5)
Lickhill Primary School, Stourport On Severn

Harvey

H appy

A dventurous

R acy

V aliant

E xcellent

Y ummy.

Harvey Gable (5)
Lickhill Primary School, Stourport On Severn

Mia Walton

M arvellous

I like sweets

A mazing

W icked

A good friend

L ovely

T alkative

O K

N oisy.

Mia Walton (6)
Lickhill Primary School, Stourport On Severn

Naomi

N ice

A mazing

O h so beautiful

M unchy

I tchy.

Naomi Griffiths (5)
Lickhill Primary School, Stourport On Severn

Owen Roser

O range

W itch

E motional

N ice

R uns

O utstanding

S o super

E gypt

R adio.

Owen Roser (5)
Lickhill Primary School, Stourport On Severn

Lauren

L ovely

A wesome

U nique

R un

E ducated

N ice.

Lauren Phillips (6)
Lickhill Primary School, Stourport On Severn

The Wild West

W ild West is the best!

I like the natives

L ook at those wild flowers!

D ancing on the hot boiling sand

W ild West is on the west side

E very buffalo is furry

S ee the natives dance

T oo many cowboys, they are fighting!

Madison Walton-Neville (7)
Marston Green Infant School, Marston Green

Cowboys

Cowboys are very wild in the west!

Ooo, buffalo skull!

Wow! Look, big, sandy and tall mountains

Buffalo are tasty!

Oh my, look food!

You are very thirsty!

See the cacti!

Ashleigh Hill (7)
Marston Green Infant School, Marston Green

Wild West

West is where it is

I like the natives

Look at those lizards on their feet

Dancing in the yellow sand

Wicked cowboys trying to steal the land

Exploring the middle of the west

See the snake slithering

The teepees are built to live inside.

Aimee Lydon (6)
Marston Green Infant School, Marston Green

Wild West

W ild West is the best!

I like the natives

L ook at those lizards

D ancing on the hot sand

W ater washing in your ears

E xplore the wild

S ee the snakes slithering around

T ime to eat the buffalo.

Elizabeth Oakes (6)
Marston Green Infant School, Marston Green

Cowboys

C owboys ride on horses!

O n the teepees are patterns!

W e hunt for Indians!

B uffalo are tasty!

O n the Indians are red bands!

Y ellow sunshine shining down!

Jake Ballinger
Marston Green Infant School, Marston Green

Cowboy

C owboys are totally wild!

O w, the snake bit me!

W owee! Riding a horse is great fun!

B uffalo are very important but also charge!

O h, look at that dancing lizard!

Y ou've gotta go to the Wild West!

Madison Kelly (6)
Marston Green Infant School, Marston Green

Strong Ben

B en is strong

E xtremely good

N uts, crazy

J elly Ben

A mazing

M ad dog Ben

I ndestructable

N ice.

Benjamin Stokes (6)
Oakfield Primary School, Rugby

Being Happy

E xciting to learn

M aths is brilliant

I get excited to go to a party

L ove snow to build a snowman

Y o-yos are fun to play with

M agnificent friends

A good friend

E lizabeth and Eloise are my friends

L ove work

E veryone should be happy

W ork hard

I love my family

S leep well at night.

Emily-Mae Lewis (5)
Oakfield Primary School, Rugby

My Friend

F izza is my best friend

R unning with my friends

I like everyone

E very day I want to play with my friend

N ow I wish to play with my friends every day

D o I want to dance with my friend?

Yasmine Sarah Bates (6)
Rykneld Primary School, Branston

A Friend

F riends are good

R un with your friend

I want to help you

E verybody come here

N o smacking

D o you like me?

Leah Beech (5)
Rykneld Primary School, Branston

A Friend

F riends that play

R un with you forever

I f somebody hurts you, you be kind

E verybody be kind

N obody hits you

D o not hit him.

Elliot Locker (5)
Rykneld Primary School, Branston

A Friend

F riendly

R eally best friend

I am a good friend

E veryone is a good friend

N ice

D o have dinner with a friend.

Fabian Purvis (6)
Rykneld Primary School, Branston

A Friend

F riends

R un together

I like to play with toys

E veryone is friends

N ew friends

D on't hurt friends.

Jacob Nicholls (5)
Rykneld Primary School, Branston

A Friend

F riendly

R eally nice

I can play

E veryone is kind

N ice

D elightful.

Joshua Smith (6)
Rykneld Primary School, Branston

My Friend

F riends are good

R unning together

I 'm playing with my friends

E veryone plays with me

N ice to play with my friends

D o you want to play with me?

Jay Palmer (6)
Rykneld Primary School, Branston

My Friend

F riends are very happy together

R unning to win first

I like to do fun things with my friends

E very day it is fun to play, fun! Fun!

N ice to get together

D ancing is great.

Samuel Gill (5)
Rykneld Primary School, Branston

My Friend

F riends are funny

R unning races

I like playing tig

E verybody dances together

N ice friends love me

D o you want to play every day?

Cameron Hollis (6)
Rykneld Primary School, Branston

My Friend

F riends are playing

R unning together

I like playing with my friends

E verybody writes

N ice playing with friends

D o you like dancing?

Leah Morris-Pajor (5)
Rykneld Primary School, Branston

A Friend

F riends play nicely

R un with your friend

I t makes you happy

E njoy playing with your friend

N o fighting

D on't hit your friend.

Jack Triptree (6)
Rykneld Primary School, Branston

My Friend

F riends are lovely

R eally nice people are friends

I play with my friends every day

E van and George are my best friends

N ow do you want to play spies?

D ancing with Evan, George and Brandon is fun.

Joshua Nicol (6)
Rykneld Primary School, Branston

My Friend

F riends are for playing with

R un on the beach

I like running with my friend

E very time I feel lonely I find my friend

N ice friend

D o you want to play with me?

Abigail Birks (5)
Rykneld Primary School, Branston

My Friend

F riends are fun

R unning in the playground is fun

I like playing with my friends

E very time I play

N ice friends play with me

D o you want to play with me?

Kaliyah Morant-Hudson (6)
Rykneld Primary School, Branston

A Friend

F riend who helps

R un with your friend

I like playing with my friend

E verybody is my friend

N o punching

D o not punch.

Zak Russell (6)
Rykneld Primary School, Branston

A Friend

F riendly with friends

R eally kind

I share with friends

E verybody is friends

N ice to friends

D o you want to come to my house?

Samuel Jones (5)
Rykneld Primary School, Branston

Lion

L ovely long hair

I ncisor teeth which rip the meat

O pens wide to hear the roar

N ose that sniffs to find its meat.

Abigail Rose Fisher (5)
Rykneld Primary School, Branston

The Tractor

T ough and strong

R umbling engines working hard

A lways remember your hard hat

C overed in mud

T urning around, moving rubbish with its big claw

O ver bumpy fields with their giant wheels

R ubble from buildings they've knocked down

S cooping up earth easily.

Kian Hicks (5)
Rykneld Primary School, Branston

Farm

F ood we eat for our tea

A nimals that we like to play with

R iding on a tractor

M ilking the cows.

Mia Gallimore (4)
Rykneld Primary School, Branston

Cake

C overed in chocolate

A nd sprinkles on top

K eep it for tomorrow?

E at it all up!

Douglas Simpson (5)
Rykneld Primary School, Branston

Little Owl

Little owl, little owl
In the dark, flying through the park
The owl is so happy and hoots
The eyes open wide
Like diamonds in the sky
Every feather flying

On the alert for bird food
With daylight breaking
Little owl falls to sleep.

Grace Holden (5)
Rykneld Primary School, Branston

My Favourite Hero

Bruce Wayne is my name
At night I am Batman
The batmobile is my car
My suit has armour and a mask
Another villain stopped
Now he will spend time in jail.

Bailey Roddis (4)
Rykneld Primary School, Branston

Horses

H orses moving through the woods

O wner riding fast

R unning up the hill

S kipping to the farm

E ating lots and lots of hay

S leeping on the hay.

Courtney Alexander (4)
Rykneld Primary School, Branston

Frogs

F lies whoosh in my mouth

R *ibbit, ribbit, ribbit*

O n the leaves I jump on a lily pad

G reen slimy skin

S ticky tongue.

Samuel Ashley (5)
Rykneld Primary School, Branston

Monkey

M y friend is cheeky

O ff he swings through the trees

N ow and then he jumps

K eeping hold with his tail

E ating as he goes

Y ellow bananas and fruit.

Seán Kinsella (5)
Rykneld Primary School, Branston

Cat

C all him and he comes

A lways hungry

T ugs at toys.

Skye Louise Holden (5)
Rykneld Primary School, Branston

Bear

B ig and brown

E ats a lot

A re furry

R oaming around the woods.

Kieran McKenna (5)
Rykneld Primary School, Branston

Rooster

R ooster wakes everybody up

O n the roof he cock-a-doodle-dos

O ut all day walking round and round

S un goes down rooster goes home

T ime to eat then to sleep

E arly in the morning when the sun rises rooster wakes up

R ed feathers on his head, on his wings, on his neck,

on his body and on his feet.

James Edward Spencer (5)
Rykneld Primary School, Branston

Rabbit

R unning rabbit through the field

A little twitching nose

B ob tails bouncing up and down

B urrows are our home

I n the fields they eat the grass

T eeth are large and healthy.

Molly Gladwin (5)
Rykneld Primary School, Branston

My Naughty Dog, Angel!

D igs in the garden

O n my bed she sleeps

G rowls at the postman.

Macey Sworder (5)
Rykneld Primary School, Branston

Football

F ocus

O n the ball

O ver the net

T ackle

B alance

A ttention

L ight work

L ength of pitch.

Joshua Harcombe Bricknell (4)
Rykneld Primary School, Branston

Dog

D ogs bark loud

O n the police force dogs help

G o running after bones.

Kaleemullah Ajmal (4)
Rykneld Primary School, Branston

Pig

P ink smooth skin

I n muddy puddles

G runting happily.

Phoebe Argent Matthews (5)
Rykneld Primary School, Branston

Tiger

T eeth like a dinosaur

I t has sharp claws

G oes roar!

E ats wild pigs

R uns fast.

Sufiya Eve Sutherland (4)
Rykneld Primary School, Branston

Kitten

K ind stroking makes them purr

I t's a type of tiger

T ail is fluffy and twitchy

T hey try to say they like it when they purr

E yes are green, little pink nose, short fluffy ears

N aps on the rug near the fire.

Jasmine Wright (5)
Rykneld Primary School, Branston

About Me - Tayla

T antrums, no way

A merica was amazing

Y ou're right, because I am tired

L ong, lovely hair

A ge 7.

Tayla Mansell (7)
St Catherine Of Siena Catholic Primary School, Lee Bank

My Name

I nayah

N oisy snakes

A pple

Y o-yo

A eroplane

H appy

A nt

S miling

A ngel

D ora.

Inayah Asad (4)
St Catherine Of Siena Catholic Primary School, Lee Bank

Why I Like Apples

I like apples

L icking the juices

I n delight

K eeping the skin on

E at all of it

A pple is juicy

P ick and mix

P lease eat one a day

L eaving the core

E at the healthy way!

O'Shea Kelly (6)
St Catherine Of Siena Catholic Primary School, Lee Bank

Christmas

C hristmas

H imself as a

R eward so that

I ndividuals know the

S acrifices

T hat He did for

M ankind to

A chieve the gift of

S alvation

D inner is great fun on Christmas Day

A pples are juicy too

Y es, I love Christmas Day.

Damilola David Oluyeye (5)
St Catherine Of Siena Catholic Primary School, Lee Bank

Teacher

T eaches me good things

E very single day

A ll through the year

C ares for me

H elps me in my work

E ach day with her is fun

R eal fun indeed.

Sheikh Mbowe (6)
St Catherine Of Siena Catholic Primary School, Lee Bank

Mother

M other makes lovely cakes

O ften gives me lots of kisses and hugs

T ears she shed to save me

H er heart of purest gold

E ager for us to tidy our room

R ead us stories day and night.

Gibril Mbowe (4)
St Catherine Of Siena Catholic Primary School, Lee Bank

My Name

D is for Deneya, that is my name

E nergetic

N ice

E njoys swimming

Y ellow is one of my favourite colours

A ll I do is play.

Deneya Rowe (6)
St Catherine Of Siena Catholic Primary School, Lee Bank

Happy

H aving fun

A pples make me happy

P laying with my friends

P laying with family

Y ou make me happy.

Ibrahim Njie (4)
St Catherine Of Siena Catholic Primary School, Lee Bank

St Catherine's

S chool

T ime

C reative

A rt

T oys

H appiness

E ducation

R ole play

I magination

N umeracy

E ating

S miling.

Shelby Loth (4)
St Catherine Of Siena Catholic Primary School, Lee Bank

Annicia

A nnicia Richards is amazing

N ever shy

N ice in every way

I ncredible and sensitive

C onsiderate and loving

I s always active

A lways laughing.

Annicia Richards (5)
St Catherine Of Siena Catholic Primary School, Lee Bank

All About Me

H appy most of the time

A lways running

R elaxes well

V ery kind

E ats a lot

Y et is very slim

B eing helpful

E njoys playing on the Xbox

L ikes to play with my cat, Charlie

L ikes Ben 10.

Harvey Bell (5)
St Catherine Of Siena Catholic Primary School, Lee Bank

Paris

P lay with my friends

A fter my homework

R eally likes to work

I have long hair

S weets are my favourite.

Paris Williams (5)
St Catherine Of Siena Catholic Primary School, Lee Bank

Squirrels

S quirrels were in my backyard playing

'Q uiet,' I said to my mom and dad

U nder the tree there was a cat watching

I tiptoed to take a closer look at them

R abbit hops up to watch as well

'R apsy, Rapsy,' said the rabbit

'E njoying the show?' said the cheeky squirrels

L oving every moment, they all went home happily.

Kaylia Gooden (7)
St Catherine Of Siena Catholic Primary School, Lee Bank

The Circus

C lowns juggle balls

I see acrobats

R eal tightrope walker

C ool contortionist

U p goes the flower yellow and red

S ee the crowd smiling.

Bonnie Ensor Bradley
St Francis CE Primary School, Bournville

The Circus

C rying at the circus

I t is the best

R abbits at the circus

C ircus is the best

U mbrellas falling on me

S oon we have got to go.

Hope Mellor (6)
St Francis CE Primary School, Bournville

The Circus

C ome to the circus

I like the circus

R ide your bike to the circus

C limb the tight rope

U p goes the umbrella

S ee the circus.

Jack Rose (6)
St Francis CE Primary School, Bournville

The Circus

C lowns are brilliant

I am amazed

R ain is tipping down in the circus

C ontortionists are good

U oops I fell over

S o I went home.

Sophie Neal (6)
St Francis CE Primary School, Bournville

The Circus

C lowns juggling balls

I went to the circus

R abbits are in the circus

C ircus is the best

U mbrellas dripping

S am went to the circus.

Hannah Le Tissier (6)
St Francis CE Primary School, Bournville

Circus

C ircus is the best

I like the circus

R un to the circus

C ircus is the best in the whole world

U p the circus is a tightrope

S illy clowns.

Jake Phillips (6)
St Francis CE Primary School, Bournville

The Circus

C ircus is fun

I like the circus

R ed clowns juggle

C ircus, I like the circus

U can come to the circus

S ongs, I like songs.

Oliver Gause (5)
St Francis CE Primary School, Bournville

The Circus

C ontortionist!

I like the circus

R abbits

C lowns

U mbrellas

S am likes the circus.

Freddie Chatterley (5)
St Francis CE Primary School, Bournville

The Circus

C lowns like to juggle and play

I like the circus

R ed noses

C ome to the circus, stars falling from the sky

U mbrellas

S ophie likes the circus.

Maryam Bandukda (6)
St Francis CE Primary School, Bournville

The Circus

C lowns like to juggle

I sabel was too early for the circus

R abbits go to the circus

C ircus is one of the best places

U p high in the sky the tent is

S am was late for the circus.

Fynn Rose (6)
St Francis CE Primary School, Bournville

Ben 10

B en 10 is the best . . .

E verybody likes Ben 10

N ever dies

T he strong superhero

E ats fish

N ever is he safe.

Niamh O'Neill (6)
St Martin De Porres RC Primary School, Moseley

Ben 10

B rilliant and brave

E veryone's best friend

N ot afraid of anyone

T he best

E njoys fighting evil

N obody stop him.

Tate Morgan (5)
St Martin De Porres RC Primary School, Moseley

Superman

§ uperman is brave and strong

U nder a bridge he can fly

P eople get saved by Superman

E veryone is safe

R ed and blue is his costume

M any people do not know who he is

A man and a superhero

N obody knows his secret.

Zak Iman, Raheem Mohammed, Freddie & Sonia Sohal (6)
St Martin De Porres RC Primary School, Moseley

Spider-Man

§ pider-Man is strong and brave

P eople don't know who Spider-Man is

I really like Spider-Man

D o not cause trouble

E veryone is saved by Spider-Man

R eady for your mission Spider-Man?

M akes webs to trap the baddies

A superhero, a spider is his badge

N ever scared, always helpful.

Keniah Downie, Cecily Webb & Armaan Hussain (6)
St Martin De Porres RC Primary School, Moseley

Ben 10

B en 10 is on fire

E scaping baddies

N ever gives up

T he superstar hero

E very day he changes

N eeds super powers.

Daniel Wootten
St Martin De Porres RC Primary School, Moseley

Ben 10

B en 10 changes into aliens

E very day fights nasty people

N ice to his family

T he boy superhero

E scapes to fight the baddies

N ever scared.

Sophie Evans (6)
St Martin De Porres RC Primary School, Moseley

Forest Schools

F un

O utdoors

R un

E xplore

S nack

T ree

S afe

C ook

H urt

O nce

O pen

L ovely

S quirrel.

Natalie Antwi
St Matthew's CE Primary School, Telford

Forest Schools

F orest School is really fun

O utside is fun at Forest Schools

R unning outside is fun at Forest Schools

E veryone has fun at Forest Schools

S ometimes it snows at Forest Schools

T ogether at Forest Schools is great

S uper we are at Forest Schools

C limb over some logs at Forest Schools

H ave fun at Forest Schools

O ak trees are fun at Forest Schools

O ver logs we climb at Forest Schools

L ove forest, we like at Forest Schools

S uper Forest School's outside.

Holly Eve Bicker (6)
St Matthew's CE Primary School, Telford

Forest Schools

F orest School is fun

O h we jump over logs

R un

E xcellent

S andwich

T ree

S nail

C hair

H at

O range

O wl

L emons

S ix.

Kian Green
St Matthew's CE Primary School, Telford

Gregory

G regory wears glasses

R eads books

E veryone knows me

G reat at numbers

O rdinary

R aced at the party

Y ear 1.

Gregory Mackie (5)
St Peter's Catholic First School, Bromsgrove

Maddie

M addie has a best friend Isobel

A pples are my favourite

D oesn't like getting up

D oes like dressing up

I like pancakes

E llie is my best friend.

Madelaine Sharpe (5)
St Peter's Catholic First School, Bromsgrove

111

Leo

L ovely

E asy to look after

O ften nice.

Leo Cadman (6)
St Peter's Catholic First School, Bromsgrove

Ellie

E xciting

L ikes pizza

L ikes pink

I like the sun

E verybody likes me.

Ellie Male (5)
St Peter's Catholic First School, Bromsgrove

Ellie

E llie is lovely

L ikes playing

L oves my brother

I love pizza

E llie is amazing.

Ellie Wright (5)
St Peter's Catholic First School, Bromsgrove

Hana

H ana is happy

A nd smiley

N o one can upset me

A nd a big cheese smile.

Hana Searle (5)
St Peter's Catholic First School, Bromsgrove

Jenson

J enson likes jelly

E veryone plays with me

N o one makes me cross

S neaky Jenson

O ranges are my favourite

N o one can upset me.

Jenson Till (5)
St Peter's Catholic First School, Bromsgrove

Isobel

I have a brother, Jack

S ophie is my best friend

O ranges are my favourite

B est

E xciting

L ovely Isobel.

Isobel Randle (5)
St Peter's Catholic First School, Bromsgrove

George

@ eorge likes to growl

E njoys dressing up as Superman

O ut and about

R ain I like

@ ive gifts

E nergetic.

George Roke (5)
St Peter's Catholic First School, Bromsgrove

Joseph

J oseph likes jelly

O ther children do too!

S un is so hot

E veryone likes the summer

P eas are my favourite

H ome is fun.

Joseph Berreen Worrall (5)
St Peter's Catholic First School, Bromsgrove

Elisha

E verybody likes me

L oves Mummy and Daddy

I like pink

S unshine is my favourite

H ave a best friend

A nd her name is Polly.

Elisha Giles (6)
St Peter's Catholic First School, Bromsgrove

Isaac

I like cakes

S pence is my last name

A mazing

A live

C ook food with Mummy.

Isaac Spence (6)
St Peter's Catholic First School, Bromsgrove

Miles

M iles likes lovely crumble

I am marvellous

L ovely Miles

E nergetic Miles

S peedy Miles.

Miles Thompson (6)
St Peter's Catholic First School, Bromsgrove

Hedgehogs

H edgehogs are nocturnal

E ating worms

D igging in the garden

G etting food

E yes black

H edgehogs curl into a ball

O utside

G oing to have some fun

S piky hedgehogs drink water.

Corban Allen (5)
St Peter's Catholic First School, Bromsgrove

Night

N obody likes the dark

I t is dark at night

G ood sky turn dark

H edgehogs come out at night

T he people sleep at night.

Alice Watkins (5)
St Peter's Catholic First School, Bromsgrove

Elisha

E is my favourite letter

L ucy is my best friend

I don't like ink

S and is like water

H olly is my sister

A pple come outside for snack time.

Elisha Robinson (5)
St Peter's Catholic First School, Bromsgrove

Torch

T orches give out light

O nly at night

R ays of light

C ome on get your torch and put it on

H old your torch under the bed and put it on.

Ethan Twamley (6)
St Peter's Catholic First School, Bromsgrove

Night

N ight is dark

I nk is dark

G rass is green

H edgehogs come out at night

T eeth can grow.

Sophie Randle (5)
St Peter's Catholic First School, Bromsgrove

The Night

N ow it is dark and time to go to bed

I am scared in the night

G o to sleep when it is bedtime

H ave your torch at night

T orches are good at night.

Jacob Newbold (5)
St Peter's Catholic First School, Bromsgrove

Night

N ight is when we go to sleep

I nk is black like the dark

G od made the night animals

H edgehogs come out at night

T orches light up the dark.

Matthew MacPherson (6)
St Peter's Catholic First School, Bromsgrove

Owls

O wls like mice

W hite and brown

L isten and find food

S woop in the dark.

Ella Mayo-Higgins (5)
St Peter's Catholic First School, Bromsgrove

The Night

N ow it's dark, it's bedtime

I wear my pyjamas

G o up the stairs

H ave my story

T eddy night-night.

Liam Lewis (5)
St Peter's Catholic First School, Bromsgrove

Torch

T hey light the dark

O utside it's dark

R uns out of charge

C annot see without it

H old it tight.

Sean Ryan (5)
St Peter's Catholic First School, Bromsgrove

The Darkness

D ark spooky trees in the pitch-black sky, owls hooting in the distance

A mazing fireworks popping in the peaceful sky

R ats scurrying across the floor in the street

K ittens snoring in bed.

Albie Murtagh (6)
Shipston On Stour Primary School, Shipston On Stour

The Killer Night

D ancing trees in the night's fresh air

A t midnight, people fast asleep in their beds

R ising foxes rising up from the wall like the king of the jungle

K iller owls swooping through the trees, whilst bowing their heads.

Adam Nash (7)
Shipston On Stour Primary School, Shipston On Stour

Light

L ight is so shiny and sparkling and it makes me feel wonderful

I ncredible, shimmering, exploding colours of flaming fireworks

G limmering sunlight shimmering on the trees

H alo surrounding the flashing round sun

T winkling starlight through the night sky.

Antonia Fairbourn (7)
Shipston On Stour Primary School, Shipston On Stour

Light

L ight is shimmering, it glows behind the moon

I ncredible fireworks exploding in the colourful bright sky

G orgeous bright flames dropping sparks at you

H eat coming from the fiery sun

T winkling flashing starlight in the spooky night sky.

Anna Hartley
Shipston On Stour Primary School, Shipston On Stour

Light

L ight as the burning bright sun in the beautiful blue sky

I ncredible sparkling flashing colours of fireworks in the night sky

G lowing as silently as the moon in the gloomy sky

H eat from the bright shining sun

T winkling sparkling sun in the fantastic sky.

Joby Morris (7)
Shipston On Stour Primary School, Shipston On Stour

Light

L ight as the sun shining down on you

I ncredible exploding fireworks in front of the moon

G lowing as silently as the moon slowly spinning

H eat of the sun warming my toes

T winkling stars shimmering down onto Earth.

Oscar Rutherford (7)
Shipston On Stour Primary School, Shipston On Stour

Light

L ight is the shining sun shimmering above the deep, blue sea

I t is incredible exploding fireworks flashing high above

G limmering sun shining on us and warming our toes

H eat of the bright sun sparkling on my skin

T he bright sun glittering on the ground.

Katelind Wilson
Shipston On Stour Primary School, Shipston On Stour

Light

L ight as the shining sun in the bright sky

I ncredible fireworks flashing in the dark, gloomy sky

G lowing softly like the moon in the inky sky

H eat from the bright sun warms the Earth

T he shimmering sun was shining on me!

Martha Thompson (6)
Shipston On Stour Primary School, Shipston On Stour

Sea

S wishing, waving fish

E el fish dancing

A nd a sea horse moving backwards and forwards.

Lexie Brain (5)
Snitterfield Primary School, Snitterfield

Oceans And Seas

O ctopus opening his mouth

C lawing crabs under the sea

E els eating fish

A swirly sea horse swims in the sea

N o divers swim with shouting sharks

S eeing the sea in the sunshine

A diving diver swimming in the sea

N o dizzy dolphins go near the sharks

D olphins diving in the sea

S eals see the sun

E very baby turtle is cute

A cute baby dolphin swimming in the sea

S inking seals swallowing sea horses.

Zoe Billiard (6)
Snitterfield Primary School, Snitterfield

Seals

S eeing the seals swimming in the sea

E ating fish and enjoying themselves

A fish comes along and waves its tail

L ying asleep, sweet dreams seals

S eeing the sunset sinking down.

Tabitha Morris (7)
Snitterfield Primary School, Snitterfield

Ocean

O ceans are salty

C oming over here

E nding at the seaside, what a wonderful place

A nd all the sea creatures

N ever let babies go in deep water.

Oliver Reilly (6)
Snitterfield Primary School, Snitterfield

Seals

S ome seals swim

E very seal can breathe under the sea

A nd the seals came by

L ots of seals were coming back

S ome seals can find a hiding place.

Max Herring (6)
Snitterfield Primary School, Snitterfield

Sea

S tarfish have little legs

E very fish is swimming fast

A ll fish are not the same.

Joshua Bull (6)
Snitterfield Primary School, Snitterfield

Seals

S wimming in the sea and enjoying themselves

E very seal has whiskers

A nd they can play ball

L egs of seals move

S eals are great.

Ella Benn (6)
Snitterfield Primary School, Snitterfield

Oceans

O ctopus swam here

C oming in colourful colours

E lectric eels flash

A fire in the sea

N othing in the sea

S uddenly they all swim back!

Saskia Foy (6)
Snitterfield Primary School, Snitterfield

Birthday Party

B alloons bursting

I nvitations going out

R obot Meccano in your present

T ehe diddly do ye ho!

H ide-and-seek, having lots of fun

D addy and Mummy cooking cakes

A rchie marching in a conga line

Y ellow cakes are ready too

P arty time for everyone

A rching back, ready to play

R e he doddly way

T asha dancing to musical statues, I

Y earn that toy. It is ace! Bye!

Archie Webb (7)
The Elms School, Colwall

Birthday Party

B alloons banging and popping

I n the house

R oaring children running around having fun

T reasure tea

H ide-and-seek at my party

D elightful dancing

A rchie age 7

Y ummy yellow biscuit

P erfect present

A melia playing party games

R adiant faces

T reats at home time

Y es!

Amelia Broughton (6)
The Elms School, Colwall

Birthday Party

B urning candles

I n the cake

R unning round the house

T ime for party food

H ot dogs and flapjacks

D elightful dancing

A nd films to watch

Y ummy yellow cupcakes

P laytime

A nimal balloons at the show

R eally fun games

T o play

Y eah!

Sophie Roberts (7)
The Elms School, Colwall

Victorians

V ictoria was Queen

I ce cream was invented by Jacob Fusselli

C harles Dickens wrote 'A Christmas Carol'.

T hey had penny farthings

O sborne House was their holiday house

R ail became electric

I n 1901 Victroria died

A lbert was her husband

N ine children she had

S ixty-three years she reigned as the Queen.

Hannah Dennison (6)
The Kingsley School, Leamington Spa

The Victorians

V ictoria was Queen for many years.

I nventions happened in her reign.

C ars and electricity came along.

T rains and railway tracks too.

O sborne House was her seaside home.

R iding penny farthings in the park was fun!

I f you were poor, children would be chimney sweeps -

A ll day long, up inside the dark and sooty chimneys

N urse, Florence Nightingale was the 'Lady with the Lamp'

S oldiers were helped by her in the war.

Jessica Ellis (7)
The Kingsley School, Leamington Spa

Victorians

V ictorians lived over 150 years ago

I t was the time Queen Victoria reigned (1837-1901)

C andles were used for light as there was no electricity

T ravel was on foot, by boat, horse or train

O nly rich children went to school, the poor had to work

R ailways were built to transport goods

I t was the period of Florence Nightingale the famous nurse

A lexander Graham Bell invented the telephone

N umber of people in Britain doubled from 16 million to 37 million

S oldiers were at war all over the world.

Isabella Fitches (6)
The Kingsley School, Leamington Spa

Victorians

V ictoria was the lovely Queen

I n black all the time

C onfident Queen was she

T ravelled in a horse and carriage

O ften sad

R arely happy

I nspired by reading

A ctually quite intelligent

N urse was Florence Nightingale

S oldiers called her 'Lady of the Lamp'.

Cecilia Goldwin (7)
The Kingsley School, Leamington Spa

Victorians

V ictorians wore robes

I t was in 1839

C lothes were different

T o ours today

O ur Queen was Victoria she

R an our country. She fell

I n love with

A lbert

N ever got over his death

S o history books say.

Charlotte Hay (7)
The Kingsley School, Leamington Spa

Victorians

V ictoria the Queen

I n the Victorian era

C hildren, she had many

T hey lived in Osborne House

O n their holidays

R uling the country

I s very important

A nd Florence Nightingale

N ursed all the wounded

S oldiers in the war.

Phoebe Suckling (7)
The Kingsley School, Leamington Spa

Zoe Rebeca

Z ooming, racing cars always zoom

O ranges are nice because they make me smile

E llie the elephant, that's my sister

R oaring tigers always roar

E very weekend I love to colour in

B eautiful butterflies fly around

E ngines always race with a moktorbike

C ats are black and they always sneak their food

A ct at a talent show.

Zoe Rebeca Christou (6)
Water Orton Primary School, Water Orton

Alexander

A pples are the best

L ions roar, roar!

E ggs for my tummy

X -rays are boring

A eroplanes are fast

N est, nest birds nest

D ollies are the boring toys

E lephants are big

R hinoceros is one of my favourite animals.

Alexander Figueroa Ashforth (7)
Water Orton Primary School, Water Orton

Spencer

S now is the best

P eople sometimes annoy me

E lephants are the best

N o one is annoying

C amels are orange

E ggs are tasty with my soldiers

R ides are great!

Spencer Williams (6)
Water Orton Primary School, Water Orton

James

J elly, jelly wobbling

A t home time I go to tree house

M e and my mum go to Derek's

E llie and me go to school

S eals are in the zoo.

James Kaczmarek (6)
Water Orton Primary School, Water Orton

Sky

S now, snow, I love snow

K iss mouse, chocolate mouse, I hate mouse

Y ou are my best friend, Maci, who always shares with me.

Sky Williams (6)
Water Orton Primary School, Water Orton

Jonny

J elly, jelly, wobbly jelly

O n Tuesday I had fish and chips

N ext I go upstairs and play on my PlayStation

N ext I go to the park

Y o-yo, playing with my yo-yo.

Jonny Savage-Williams (6)
Water Orton Primary School, Water Orton

Alfie

A nts are cool because they have six legs

L ibraries are good

F ire engines go nee-naw, nee-naw

I ce cream makes me go yum-yum

E lephants are cool because they go crazy like me.

Alfie Attridge (7)
Water Orton Primary School, Water Orton

Bethany Rose

B ooks fill my bookcase with colours

E lephants are covered all over my Thailand dress

T heatres show lots of ballets and plays, when I'm older I'll be in one too

H elium balloons float through the sky, making me smile

A bbie is my very best friend.

N essie is short for my mother's name who reads to me

Y oghurt is nice with strawberry jam

R ose is my favourite flower, it smells like summer days

O wls are interesting animals

S eptember's stone is blue, it is the stone of my birthday

E mily elephant is my favourite toy.

Bethany Rose Warren (7)
Water Orton Primary School, Water Orton

Ollie Taylor

O ctopuses have eight legs

L unchtime is the best

L ifeboats save people

I nsects are my favourite things

E dges

T eeth are very important

A pples are good for you

Y ears take forever

L azy cats snore all the time

O ceans are very blue

R hinos are my favourite type of animals.

Ollie Taylor (6)
Water Orton Primary School, Water Orton

Daisy

D aisies are in the ground

A t play I play with Mollie

I ce is cold and slippy

S eawater with a leopard in

Y es, yes! I like the weekend.

Daisy Wood (6)
Water Orton Primary School, Water Orton

Zac Prince

Z ooming stars in the sky

A ctivities are the best

C ircus makes me laugh

P ears make me jog along

R iding along on my bike in the park

I ce creams are very, very cold!

N ice science makes me happy

C omputers are sunny

E xplaining the rules for football.

Zachary Prince (6)
Water Orton Primary School, Water Orton

Tyler Matthews

T iny tigers are the best

Y ellow is the best in the world

L ots of litlte spiders running round

E lephants are fat

R ainbows come when I come out

M otorbikes racing round the track

A pples on the tree

T ea time is nice

T ortoises are slow

H olly is sharp

E erie X-rays look weird

W hat a taste - yuck!

S weets taste nice.

Tyler Matthews (7)
Water Orton Primary School, Water Orton

143

Niamh Rooney

N ecklaces are beautiful, shining bright

I love my family so much

A nimals are cute

M y best friends are Lilly and Sophie

H appy birthday to me

R hinos are fine

O zzy is the best dog in the world

O range is the best

N ice rainbow up high in the sky

E agles on the trees, building their nest

Y ellow sun burning very hot.

Niamh Rooney (7)
Water Orton Primary School, Water Orton

Lauren Fleming

L ovely summer, it's my favourite season

A mber's my favourite stone

U nicorn's horns are as shiny as a star

R obins are very colourful

E ntertainment is what I like doing

N ature is a forest's life, I like making it

F estivals are one of my favourite things

L istening is what I like doing, because I get stickers

E xcellent is what I like being said to

M agazines are what I like collecting

I nteresting work is what I like doing

N ibbble is how I eat

G eography is my favourite subject.

Lauren Fleming (6)
Water Orton Primary School, Water Orton

Maci Taylor

May is my friend's birthday

Ask a teacher if you are stuck

Cars zooming past me

I love my family

Telephones ringing all day long

And ringing all night long

Yeah, yeah, I love September

Love, love is jolly

October is Halloween

Run, run, as fast as you can.

Maci Taylor (6)
Water Orton Primary School, Water Orton

My Teacher

Mrs Pickering is going to be a mummy

Ready to leave

Super and special

Posh

Is incredible

Caring for other people

Kind

Everyone will miss her

Round tummy she has

Intelligent

Never forget her

Good and graceful.

Molly Jobe (6)
Woodthorpe J&I School, Birmingham

My Teacher

M ummy-to-be

R eliable, really good teacher

S he's very kind and nice

P olite and posh

I ncredible and cheerful

C aring and special

K ind and intelligent

E veryone will miss her

R eally knowledgeable and pleasant

I rreplaceable and interesting

N ever rude or unkind, I want to say

G ood luck Mrs Pickering.

Jack Carter (6)
Woodthorpe J&I School, Birmingham

Mrs Pickering

M rs Pickering is special

R osy cheeks has she

S oon she is having a baby

P eople are going to miss her

I will too

C aring for us children

K ind to everyone

E njoy her lessons, they are fun

R eally lovely teacher

I n every way

N ow your baby is ready to come out

G ood luck on your special day.

Megan Rankin (7)
Woodthorpe J&I School, Birmingham

Mrs Pickering

M rs Pickering, mum-to-be

R unning is her favourite

S pecial to me

P olite

I ntelligent

C osy

K nowledgeable

E ver so kind

R ound belly

I nteresting

N ice

G ood at PE.

Tarell Stokes (6)
Woodthorpe J&I School, Birmingham

Mrs Pickering

M rs Pickering is

R eady to have her baby

S he is a special teacher

P eople say that she is polite and kind

I ntelligent and irreplaceable

C aring and careful

K nows a lot of knowledge

E verybody will miss her

R elentless in being nice

I nterested in PE

N obody will forget her

G raceful and great.

Riya Dharmadhikari (7)
Woodthorpe J&I School, Birmingham

Mrs Pickering

Mrs Pickering likes PE

Ready to have a baby

She is posh

People like her

I like her as well

Come and see us again Mrs Pickering

Kind every day

Excellent every day

Reliable every day

I like her

Nice to everybody

Graceful.

Matthew Bingham (7)
Woodthorpe J&I School, Birmingham

Mrs Pickering

M rs Pickering is going to be a mummy

R eally likes to have fun

S he is super

P eople are going to miss her

I am going to cry

C ome back

K ind and helpful

E veryone wants to see her

R eally soon

I rreplaceable

N eed her back

G ood luck.

Ryan Dunne (6)
Woodthorpe J&I School, Birmingham

Mrs Pickering

M rs Pickering likes PE

R eady

S he is having a baby

P eople

I ntelligent

C areful

K ind

E asy to like

R ound tummy

I nterested

N obody

G raceful.

Jack Kite (6)
Woodthorpe J&I School, Birmingham

Mrs Pickering

M y teacher Mrs Pickering is

R eady to have a baby.

S he is

P erfect for a teacher.

I want her to stay for a

C ouple more weeks as I

K now I will miss her

E very day. I hope she is

R eally happy and her baby

I s not

N aughty, but

G reat like her!

George Callus (6)
Woodthorpe J&I School, Birmingham

155

Mrs Pickering

M rs Pickering, my class teacher, is getting

R eady to have a baby

S he is coming back next year

P eople will be sorry to see her go

I shall miss her but will not

C ry

K een to see her back, will

E specially

R eally work hard, learning new and interesting things

I will never be

N aughty with Miss Taylor

G ood news Mrs Pickering has had the baby!

Imaan Riaz (7)
Woodthorpe J&I School, Birmingham

Mrs Pickering

M rs Pickering is going to be a mum

R eally brave

S he is so super special

P olite and pleasant

I ntelligent

C areful

K ind,

E asy to like

R ound tummy

I nteresting

N o need for fuss

G raceful and great.

Hashim Masood (6)
Woodthorpe J&I School, Birmingham

Mrs Pickering

M rs Pickering is a mummy-to-be

R eally kind, rocks all the time

S mart and helpful

P leasant and posh

I ntelligent

C areful

K nowledgeable

E njoy her lessons

R eally calm

I nteresting

N eeds some help

G reat.

Grace Bradley (6)
Woodthorpe J&I School, Birmingham

Mrs Pickering

M ummy-to-be

R eally good teacher

S he's proud of herself

P osh

I ntelligent

C aring teacher

K a-ching

E asy teacher

R eady to have her baby

I n a good mood

N ever a bad teacher

G ood.

Jack-Daniel Dyson (7)
Woodthorpe J&I School, Birmingham

Mrs Pickering

M rs Pickering

R eally nice

S pecial teacher

P olite

I ntelligent

C aring

K ind

E njoys PE

R eliable

I mportant

N eat

G ood.

Rhia Jackson (7)
Woodthorpe J&I School, Birmingham

The New Baby

M rs Pickering is going to have a baby, I am

R eally, really pleased because

S he is so special

P E is her favourite lesson

I will really miss her. The

C lass will be sad. I hope she

K eeps in touch

E veryone wants to see her baby when she comes

R ound to our class

I think she will be a good mom. My

N ew teacher is called Miss Taylor. She is

G oing to take care of us.

Freya Snipe (6)
Woodthorpe J&I School, Birmingham

Mrs Pickering

M ummy-to-be
R eliable
S pecial

P olite
I ntelligent
C areful
K ind
E asy
R ound tummy
I nteresting
N eeds a rest
G raceful.

Harry Bull (6)
Woodthorpe J&I School, Birmingham

Mrs Pickering Is Having A Baby

M ummy-to-be
R eally reliable
S uper special

P E is fun with Mrs Pickering
I s intelligent
C areful Mrs Pickering
K ind
E xtra easy
R ound belly
I n hospital
N eeds nobody
G rateful.

Patrick McCormack (6)
Woodthorpe J&I School, Birmingham

My Pet Dog

Mad Tess barks at the postman

You can hear her growling

Party time, Tess likes to eat sausages

Every day we have fun with Tess

Tess is a good dog. We love her very much

Daft and funny, a happy dog

Ooooooh! She howls

Great dog, eats all her food

Tess has been good today

Extremely friendly and nice

She tries to sleep in the warmest place

She is a happy dog.

Nia Thomas (6)
Worthen CE Primary School, Worthen

My Pet Dog

M y pet dog, Tazz, fun to play with

Y oung, only four years old, jumping like a puppy

P erfect dog, best in the world

E ven better than a horse

T azz loves bones . . . not fluffy toys

D roopy ears, which flap about

O dd, curly tail that wags

'G et off the sofa!' we shout

T azz gets frightened sometimes

A fraid of big, growling dogs

Z igzagging in and out of the garden

Z ipping behind the bushes.

Cerys Buxton (7)
Worthen CE Primary School, Worthen

Ben

My pal Ben is great

Yellow is his favourite colour

Brilliant at football, his favourite sport

Elephant is his favourite animal

Spaghetti is his favourite food

Team he likes the best is England

Favourite hobby - watching telly

Runs faster than me

I like him a lot

Eager to eat his dinner

Naughty sometimes

Dangerous sometimes.

Thomas Adkins (7)
Worthen CE Primary School, Worthen

My Friend Beth

M y friend is so funny

Y ou can hear Beth laughing

B eing her friend is great

E very day, Beth listens

S o nicely, when I'm talking about my goldfish

T errific friend to play with

F antastic games and things to do

R eally fun and exciting

I think that Beth is brilliant

E xcellent at being quiet or loud

N ever cross or angry with me

D oing things I like.

Bethany Thomas (7)
Worthen CE Primary School, Worthen

167

My Funny Dad Is Talented

My dad shouts at Monty when he chases the cat

Yelling loudly at the dog, the cat runs off

Funny jokes when I play with him

Unlike Mum, Dad says Monty is silly

Naughty Dad, when I tell him to be good

Noisy Dad, when I tell him to be quiet

Yo-yo expert and loves to laugh

Daring and sort of silly sometimes

A bit of a daydreamer as well

Dad is almost always outside gardening

I'd never wish for a better dad

Sometimes I wish he was home more

The best thing about Dad is his smile

A lot of jokes and a lot of fun

Late at night when he comes home

Every day spent with Dad is fantastic!

Neat and tidy when he's off to work

Today, he will be working very hard

Every time he comes home we hug lots

Days are great when Dad's at home.

Lily Pembroke (7)
Worthen CE Primary School, Worthen

Jane, My Toy

J ane is my favourite toy doll

A nd she even comes to bed

N ext to me under the warm blankets

E verywhere she goes even to Centre Parcs!

M y toy doll, Jane, has a pink stripy dress

Y ou can see a red heart in the middle

T wo purple shoes with yellow laces

O range, floppy summer hat

Y ou would like her so much.

Charlotte Lewis (6)
Worthen CE Primary School, Worthen

169

Young Writers Information

We hope you have enjoyed reading this book - and that you will continue to enjoy it in the coming years.

If you like reading and writing poetry drop us a line, or give us a call, and we'll send you a free information pack.

Alternatively if you would like to order further copies of this book or any of our other titles, then please give us a call or log onto our website at www.youngwriters.co.uk.

Young Writers Information
Remus House
Coltsfoot Drive
Peterborough
PE2 9BF
(01733) 890066